BOOKS BY PHILIP LEVINE

THEY FEED THEY LION

They Feed They Lion

POEMS BY

PHILIP LEVINE

NEW YORK   ATHENEUM   1978

My thanks are given to the editors of the following publications in which these poems first appeared:

THE HUDSON REVIEW (*¡Hola Miguelin!, To a Fish Head Found on the Beach Near Malaga, Coming Home, Autumn, Angel 14, Thistles*)

IOWA REVIEW (*Salami, Cry for Nothing*)

JEOPARDY (*Renaming the Kings*)

KAYAK (*The Space We Live, Saturday Sweeping, They Feed They Lion, How Much Can It Hurt*)

NEW AMERICAN REVIEW (*Robert*)

THE NEW YORKER (*The Cutting Edge, Later Still, Dark Rings, Breath*)

NORTHWEST REVIEW (*Angel Butcher, The Children's Crusade*)

PEMBROKE MAGAZINE (*Waking in Alicante*)

POETRY (*Alone, The Way Down*)

STAND (*To P.L., 1916–1937*)

UNICORN FOLIO (*Detroit Grease Shop Poem*)

UNICORN JOURNAL (*The Angels of Detroit*)

Library of Congress catalog card number 74-183612
Published simultaneously in Canada by McClelland and Stewart Ltd
Manufactured in the United States of America by
Halliday Lithograph Corporation, West Hanover and Plympton, Massachusetts
Designed by Harry Ford
First Printing January 1972
Second Printing September 1972
Third Printing February 1976
Fourth Printing March 1978

for those who helped me

especially Fran

my Lion, my Thistle, my Tree

CONTENTS

I

II

III

IV

V

I

RENAMING THE KINGS

River of green stone,
in August '62 I stuck my head in
your lap one mile south of Piedra
where you fall suddenly away
from the highway.   107
in the valley and me
going dizzy, stopped the bike
and stumbled down
over the flat, patient stone, leaned out,
and then you in my eyes,
green tatters of memory, glimpses
of my own blood flashing
like fish, the grasses
dancing calmly, one silver point
like the charmed eye of an eel.
Five hours later I wakened
with the first darkness flowing
from the river bottom
through me to stone, to
the yellow land grasses and storming
the lower branches of the eucalyptus.
I could feel the water
draining from my blood and the stone
going out—the twin bushes of the lungs
held themselves seriously
like people about to take fire,
and when the first minnows startled
I rose into the sky. We
gathered every last tendril
of blue into our breath.

I named the stone John
after my mysterious second born.
High in its banks, slashed with silver,
riding the jagged blade of heaven
down to earth, the river shouts its name.

THE SPACE WE LIVE

I

Light shrugs at the last dreams
of cops and whores. The three cold stacks
above the tire factory climb
the dawn. An old man, home from work,
sits on the bed, unlacing.
How small the space a man lives,
elbows on guard, the fingers
curled, the head tucked.

As a child I lived cupboards, drawers,
tiny hutches of straw and wax,
narrow fluted corridors
of the ear. At night I would spread
my arms and legs under the fresh sheets
and laugh to hear the first sly growls
of watch dog, the cluck of hen
in the silvery yards where mother moon waited.

I I

The stained muzzle, the tail's
nervous quivering as though
an unfelt wind stirred, the fox
floats in the heavy smell
of its living,
and the singed blades of grass
spring upward after the passing.

Crow lives the horizon of squat olives,
approves of everything, outlasts
the barn mice searching the garbage
for their death, coyote
calls at the edge of light
until the dawn blooms slowly
from the elm leaves, and nothing
moves and nothing lives
for that one space before the word is flesh.

THE CUTTING EDGE

Even the spring water
couldn't numb the slash
of that green rock
covered with river lace.
Slowly the blood spread
from under the flap of skin
that winked open; deep in
my foot, for a second, I saw
something holding back,
and I sat down in the water
up to my waist in water,
my pockets filling with it.
I squeezed the green rock,
pressed it to my cheeks,
to my eyelids. I did not
want to be sick or faint
with children looking on,
so I held to the edge of the stone
until I came back.

That was a year ago.
I threw the stone away
as though I could banish it
from creation; I threw
it into the dry reeds,
where it could do no harm,
and dragged myself bleeding
up the hillside and drove home.

I forgot the stone
drying among burned reeds
in October; I forgot
how cold this place got
when the winds came down the pass,
and how, after the late rains,
the first pale ice-plants dot

the slopes like embroidery,
then larkspur, myrtle, and the great,
bellowing, horned blooms
that bring summer on.

Huddling to where it fell,
like a stunned animal,
the stone stayed. I kneel
to it and see how dust
has caked over half of it
like a protruding lip
or a scab on no cut
but on a cutting edge.
It comes away from the ground
easily, and the dry dirt
crumbles, and it's the same.
In the river its colors
darken and divide
as though stained; the green
patterning I thought lace
is its own, and the oily shine
comes back, and the sudden smell
of dizziness and sweat.

I could take it home
and plant it in a box;
I could talk about
what it did to me
and what I did to it,
or how in its element
it lives like you or me.
But it stops me, here
on my open hand,
by being a stone, and I send
it flying over the heads
of the fishing children,
arching alone above

the dialogue of reeds,
falling and falling toward water,
somewhere in water to strike
a conversation of stone.

¡HOLA MIGUELIN!

I

The night is rising in the young grass—
before noon and the land wind
sways through the fields. Along the trunk
of each blade, a juice rising
toward the pale crown.

I shut my eyes and imagine
a black dried bough of olive.
I bend it. When it gives
with a dry cough
a fine dust rises into our nostrils.

II

She stumbles into the noon—this morning
she was a shy wife—and the young
coarse wine that numbs
her arms and cools the sweat on
her forehead is summer itself.

If she goes forward she does so
from side to side
on her long delicate legs, bearing
herself between them, a faint
musk, a crown of curls, a gift
for the night that is always rising.

ROBERT

October. From Simpson's hill
the great moon of stone
frowns in the rain. In the
fields below dark bruises
of spike stiffen into seed.
The cows are shuffling
behind me, back down
to the long chromium sheds
and the painless taking.

I watch an hour pass.
The darkness rises from
the floor of the valley
thickening the air between
branches, between stone
and tree, between my eyes
and what was here.

Now I'm in the dark.
I remember pages torn
from an automotive catalogue,
an ad once fallen from
heaven and hanging in
the city air—"It's never too late . . ."
If I follow my hands
will I feel the winter shake
the almonds into blossom?

TO A FISH HEAD FOUND ON THE BEACH NEAR MÁLAGA

I

Flat, eventless afternoon
searching among the stones for nothing
I come upon the fish head.

                              "¡Hola!"
Right off, head to head, with this
wide-eyed, unlistening remnant
of dead metal trailing its single
stiff feather of flesh.

                    We talk of loneliness,
of the fear of stones falling like rain,
hatred of water tumbling out of dreams
and filling our small rooms. Shafts of sand
sifting under doors, filming
first the glasses, then the eyes,
weighing down the lips, the cry.

II

                              Here, halfway
from home, I discover my head, its hideous
King Tongue going. My good hands explore it,
the hair thinning, the eyes scratched
and hot, that let the lids thump down,
and the poor muscles, unsleeping,
as burned as drawn ropes.
Only the chin happy, hidden in fur.

III

But how good to find companionship
of any kind. Fish head and man head,
communing in their tongue, an iron yawn
out over the waves, the one poem born
of the eternal and always going back.
I throw the fish head to the sea.
Let it be fish once more.

                     I sniff my fingers
and catch the burned essential oil
seeping out of death. Out of beginning,
I hear, under the sea roar, the bone words
of teeth tearing earth and sea,
anointing the tongues with stone and sand,
water eating fish, fish water,
head eating head to let us be.

SALAMI

Stomach of goat, crushed
sheep balls, soft full
pearls of pig eyes,
snout gristle, fresh earth,
worn iron of trotter, slate
of Zaragoza, dried cat heart,
cock claws. She grinds
them with one hand and
with the other fists
mountain thyme, basil,
paprika, and knobs of garlic.
And if a tooth of stink thistle
pulls blood from the round
blue marbled hand
all the better for
this ruby of Pamplona,
this bright jewel of Vich,
this stained crown
of Solsona, this
salami.
                    The daughter
of mismatched eyes,
36 year old infant smelling
of milk. Mama, she cries, mama,
but mama is gone,
and the old stone cutter
must wipe the drool
from her jumper. His puffed fingers
unbutton and point her
to toilet. Ten, twelve hours
a day, as long as the winter sun
holds up he rebuilds
the unvisited church
of San Martin. Cheep cheep
of the hammer high above
the town, sparrow cries
lost in the wind or lost

in the mind. At dusk he leans
to the coal dull wooden Virgin
and asks for blessings on
the slow one and peace
on his grizzled head, asks
finally and each night
for the forbidden, for
the knowledge of every
mysterious stone, and
the words go out on
the overwhelming incense
of salami.
                    A single crow
passed high over the house,
I wakened out of nightmare.
The winds had changed,
the Tremontana was tearing
out of the Holy Mountains
to meet the sea winds
in my yard, burning and
scaring the young pines.
The single poplar wailed
in terror. With salt,
with guilt, with the need
to die, the vestments
of my life flared, I
was on fire, a stranger
staggering through my house
butting walls and falling
over furniture, looking
for a way out. In the last room
where moonlight slanted
through a broken shutter
I found my smallest son
asleep or dead, floating
on a bed of colorless light.
When I leaned closer

I could smell the small breaths
going and coming, and each
bore its prayer for me,
the true and earthy prayer
of salami.

II

CRY FOR NOTHING

I.
Make the stream
on the hurt faces
of stones, up the hillside
into the black house
of firs. Say
your name to stump,
to silence, to the sudden wings
of the air, say
your name to yourself.
It doesn't matter cause
it all comes back
a red leaf prick
in your crotch, burr balls
tapping at your ankles
with their Me! Me!
the fresh weed tongue lashing
at your cheek
to make you cry
for nothing.

2.

Motor roar of bad clutch, passing
goats, drunk trucks,
cement haulers, night men
coming home on foot, dawn men
going out
and steaming in anger
at the cold. Mark sleeps
next to me, his blond
woman hair tangling
the gear shift, behind
the little ones
breathing in their
bad socks, farting
and gnashing at
the first sex dreams,
and the mama, my alone
woman rolling in the limbo
of sleep. I'm awake
and staring
for the first breaks of light
between the prisoned towers
of hell slums north
of Barcelona and the dark tear pools
left in the streets.

3.
He let her drive
and she crashed her poppa's
front porch. Man
asked for her license
and she 14. The evening
gathering above the wooden
roofs, a heavy darkness
spreading from car lights.
Time to go. Small kids
near the kitchen asking,
and the oven flashing
its magic. Time to go
if you got a place
to go. Man let Luther,
and he called home, her
mother say she gone
early and the baby
be coming by now and
where is he.

           He with me
pushing the old black Lincoln
back down the drive
watching the radiator bare
its muddy wounds. Luther
rolling his sleeves up
high and cupping his long
hillbilly fingers around
a flaring match, Luther
cocking his tattoo
against the black rain and
the rain of black luck, Luther
pushing on toward
the jewelled service station
of free cokes
and credit there ahead
in a heaven of blue

falling and nothing
going to make him cry
for nothing.

COMING HOME, *Detroit,* 1968

A winter Tuesday, the city pouring fire,
Ford Rouge sulfurs the sun, Cadillac, Lincoln,
Chevy gray. The fat stacks
of breweries hold their tongues. Rags,
papers, hands, the stems of birches
dirtied with words.
                              Near the freeway
you stop and wonder what came off,
recall the snowstorm where you lost it all,
the wolverine, the northern bear, the wolf
caught out, ice and steel raining
from the foundries in a shower
of human breath. On sleds in the false sun
the new material rests. One brown child
stares and stares into your frozen eyes
until the lights change and you go
forward to work. The charred faces, the eyes
boarded up, the rubble of innards, the cry
of wet smoke hanging in your throat,
the twisted river stopped at the color of iron.
We burn this city every day.

DETROIT GREASE SHOP POEM

Four bright steel crosses,
universal joints, plucked
out of the burlap sack—
"the heart of the drive train"—
the book says. Stars
on Lemon's wooden palm,
stars that must be capped,
rolled, and annointed,
that have their orders
and their commands as he
has his.
              Under the blue
hesitant light another day
at Automotive
in the city of dreams.
We're all there to count
and be counted, Lemon,
Rosie, Eugene, Luis,
and me, too young to know
this is for keeps, pinning
on my apron, rolling up
my sleeves.
              The roof leaks
from yesterday's rain,
the waters gather above us
waiting for one mistake.
When a drop falls on Lemon's
corded arm, he looks at it
as though it were something
rare or mysterious
like a drop of water or
a single lucid meteor
fallen slowly from
nowhere and burning on
his skin like a tear.

THE ANGELS OF DETROIT

I

I could hear them in fever
hovering in the closet or
falling from the mirror. I
could see them in the first dreams
of my dead.
        Perfume of scorched
clothes . . . she spits back
at the spitting iron, she slaps
it with a round pink palm
and the angels sigh
from the shadowy valleys
of my shirts.

II
I wore angels.
They saved me in the streets
where the towers hung above
suspended on breath, they
saved me from the pale woman
who smoothed the breasts
of chickens or the red-armed
one who sold bread in
the shop of knives.

While I leaned
on the cold stones of summer
and tried to cry and tried
to change they sent me
a robed mother or a
promise in the dark hall.
In the black river at midnight
they said, Go back!

They sent snow
to cover the steps, to crown
the teeth of garbage and bless
the deaths of old cars, snow
falling on our upturned faces
in the great church, the presses
choiring in the roof of night.

III
From Toledo by bus,
from Flat Rock on syphoned gas,
from the iron country on
a dare. For one night.
Stash says, Nigger
boy's crying in
the shit house.

All of us far from
momma and gettin farther.

IV
At the end of mud road
in the false dawn of the slag heap
the hut of the angel Bernard.
His brothers are factories and
bowling teams, his mother is the
power to blight, his father
moves in all men like a threat,
a closing of hands, an unkept
promise to return.

                    We talk
for years; everything we
say comes to nothing. We drink
bad beer and never lie. From
his bed he pulls fists
of poems and scatters them
like snow. "Children are guilty,"
he whispers, and the soft mouth
puffs like a wound.

He wants it all tonight.
The long hard arms of a black woman,
he wants tenderness, he wants
the power to die in the
chalice of God's tears.

True dawn through the soaped window.
The plastic storm-wrap swallows wind.
'37 Chevie hoodless, black burst
lung of inner tube, pot metal
trees buckling under sheets.
He cries to sleep.

V

In a toilet on Joy Rd
long Eddie on alto.
The yellows of his eyes
brown on pot, the brown centers
burned like washed gold.

Never knew the tune. 16
years old, drummer
had to prod him to music.
So much sorrow in hatred,
so much tenderness
he could taste coming up
from the rich earth.

Little clown. Caught all alone,
arm in a mail-box.
Never did nothing right
except tell the cops to suck
and wave them off like flies.

VI

After midnight of the final
shift, with all our prayers
unanswered, we gave up.
Unvisored pale knot of
West Virginia, mountain rock and
black valley earth, ungloved
yellow potato, dried tubers,
yoked bean, frozen cedars
of weariness, we gave up.

The cranes slip
overhead. The ore pours
from the earth to us, poor earth
somewhere unseamed. If you
listen quiet to Lonnie
next to you or hopping Sugar
you can hear it
piping in pity.

Don't matter what rare breath
puddles in fire on
the foundry floor. The toilets
overflow, the rats dance, the maggots
have it, the worms of money
crack like whips, and
among the angels
we lie down.

VII

Red haired black skinned
Cuban woman. Wait all night
in the parking lot. Doze and talk—
to no one—of home. The panels
of the black chapel flame,
the glass melts or races
with stars. Nothing lasts
forever. Sun up shatters
the yellowed windows of the old Dodge.
She meets us, coatless, in magenta,
an early flower late blooming
in the fenced white wastes,
bare arms open.

SATURDAY SWEEPING

Saturday sweeping
with an old broom
counting the strokes
back and forth.
The dust sprays
up silver in the
February sun
and comes down gray.
Soft straw muzzle
poking in and
bringing out
scraps of news,
little fingers
and signatures.
Everybody's
had this room
one time or another
and never thought
to sweep. Outside
the snows stiffen,
the roofs loosen
their last teeth
into the streets.
Outside it's
1952,
Detroit, unburned,
stumbles away
from my window
over the drained roofs
toward the river
to scald its useless
hands. Half
the men in this town
are crying in
the snow, their eyes
blackened like
Chinese soldiers.

The gates are closing
at Dodge Main
and Wyandotte
Chemical; they
must go home
to watch the kids
scrub their brown
faces or grease
cartridges for
the show down.
If anyone knocks
on your door
he'll be
oil flecked or
sea born, he'll
be bringing word
from the people
of the ice drifts
or the great talking dogs
that saved the Jews.
Meanwhile our masters
will come on
television
to ask for our help.
Here, the radiator's
working, stove says
Don't touch,
and the radio's crying,
I don't get enough.
I'm my keeper,
the only thing
I've got,
sweeping out
my one-room life
while the sun's
still up.

ANGEL BUTCHER

At sun up I am up
hosing down the outdoor abattoir
getting ready. The water
steams and hisses on the white stones
and the air pales to a
thin blue.
                    Today it is
Christophe. I don't see him
come up the long climb or
know he's here until I hear
my breathing double
and he's beside me smiling
like a young girl.
                        He asks
me the names of all
the tools and all
their functions, he lifts
and weighs and
balances, and runs a long
forefinger down the tongue
of each blade.
                    He asks
me how I came to this place and
this work, and I tell him how
I began with animals, and
he tells me how
he began with animals. We
talk about growing up and losing
the strange things we never
understood and settling.
                            I help
him with his robes; he
has a kind of modesty and sits
on the stone table with
the ends of the gown crossed
in his lap.

He wants to die
like a rabbit, and he wants me
to help him. I hold
his wrist; it's small, like
the throat of a young hen, but
cool and dry. He holds
mine and I can feel the
blood thudding in the ring
his fingers make.
                    He helps me, he
guides my hand at first. I can
feel my shoulders settle and
the bones take the weight, I can
feel my lungs flower as the
swing begins. He smiles again
with only one side of his mouth
and looks down to the
dark valley where the cities
burn. When I hit
him he comes apart like a
perfect puzzle or an
old flower.
                    And my legs
dance and twitch for hours.

THEY FEED THEY LION

Out of burlap sacks, out of bearing butter,
Out of black bean and wet slate bread,
Out of the acids of rage, the candor of tar,
Out of creosote, gasoline, drive shafts, wooden dollies,
They Lion grow.
                    Out of the gray hills
Of industrial barns, out of rain, out of bus ride,
West Virginia to Kiss My Ass, out of buried aunties,
Mothers hardening like pounded stumps, out of stumps,
Out of the bones' need to sharpen and the muscles' to stretch,
They Lion grow.
                    Earth is eating trees, fence posts,
Gutted cars, earth is calling in her little ones,
"Come home, Come home!" From pig balls,
From the ferocity of pig driven to holiness,
From the furred ear and the full jowl come
The repose of the hung belly, from the purpose
They Lion grow.
                    From the sweet glues of the trotters
Come the sweet kinks of the fist, from the full flower
Of the hams the thorax of caves,
From "Bow Down" come "Rise Up,"
Come they Lion from the reeds of shovels,
The grained arm that pulls the hands,
They Lion grow.
                    From my five arms and all my hands,
From all my white sins forgiven, they feed,
From my car passing under the stars,
They Lion, from my children inherit,
From the oak turned to a wall, they Lion,
From they sack and they belly opened
And all that was hidden burning on the oil-stained earth
They feed they Lion and he comes.

III

ALONE

Sunset, and the olive grove flames
on the far hill. We descend
into the lunging shadows
of goat grass, and the air

deepens like smoke.
You were behind me, but when I turned
there was the wrangling of crows
and the long grass rising in the wind

and the swelling tips of grain
turning to water under a black sky.
All around me the thousand
small denials of the day

rose like insects to the flaming
of an old truth, someone alone
following a broken trail of stones
toward the deep and starless river.

AUTUMN

Out of gas south
of Ecorse. In the dark
I can smell the dogs
circling behind the
wrecked cars.
          On a sidestreet,
unlighted, we find a
new Chevy. I suck
the tube until
my mouth fills
and cools with new
American wine.

———

Old man says,
Elephant moves slow, tortoise
don't hardly move at all and they
has no trouble to be
a hundrid.
          The small
ladders of hair dangle
from his nostrils, hands
peppered like old eggs.

———

I left you in Washington,
honey, and went to Philly. All the
way beside the tracks, empires
of metal shops, brickflats, storage tanks,
robbing the air.
                    Later, behind
barbed wire, I found small arms
swaddled in cosmoline, tanks, landing
craft, half tracks smiling
through lidded eyes,
grenades blooming in
their beds.
                    April,
1954, we've got each other
in a borrowed room.

———

Who comes before dawn through
the drifts of dried leaves
to my door? The clawed gopher,
the egret lost on his way, the inland
toad, the great
Pacific tortoise?
                    I rise
from a warm bed and go and
find nothing, not a neighbor
armed and ready, not a cop
not even my own son
deserting.
                    I stand
in a circle of light, my heart
pounding and pounding at the door
of its own wilderness.

———

Snow steaming on the still
warm body of the jackrabbit
shot and left, snow
on the black streets
melting, snow falling endlessly
on the great runways that
never fill.
                    The twentieth autumn
of our war, the dead heart
and the living clogged
in snow.
                    A small clearing
in the pines, the wind
talking through the high trees,
we have water, we
have air, we have bread, we have
a rough shack whitening,
we have snow on your eyelids,
on your hair.

ANGEL 14

He passes into the streets in a business suit,
he crosses at the corner where the children wait
on their way to the fenced yards and the dark barns.

The first snow falls dusting the raw faces
of the oak stumps, the first snow thickens like paste
between the slender fingers of the raccoon.

He lies face down on a rumpled bed and feels
creation ticking in his heart, ticking in his bowels,
he feels the blood and its rushing into black stones.

It's afternoon and once more the light is failing.
I won't serve, he says. His eyes are cups
that hold fists, hair pins, bombers,

the lost tooth a girl wrapped in cloth,
the old problems without solutions, the yellowing
pages read and reread, the circle drawn in dirt.

The muscles knot between my ribs, I carry an axe
and cut nothing, looking for dust I pour out milk.
Silver filings collect under fingernails,

nailed to the iron pond the egret eats its wings,
a child turns suddenly and crashes through glass
and passes into the streets in a business suit.

HOW MUCH CAN IT HURT?

The woman at the checkstand
Who wishes you cancer

The fat man who hates his mother
The doctor who forgets

The soup bubbling on the back of the stove
The stone staring into the sun

The girl who kisses her own arms
The girl who fries her hair

The egg turning brown under the spoon
The lemon laughing all night long

My brother in his uniform over Dresden
The single thrill of fire going for the bed

The kindergarten blowing its windows out
Chalk burning the little fingers

The newspaper waiting all weekend
Dozing in rain with the deaths smeared on its lips

The oiling and loading and the springing
The bullets sucking quietly in their cradles

How much can it hurt in the wood
In the long nerve of lead, in the fattened head

How much can it hurt
In each ration of meat hooked and hanging

In the unfinished letter, the dried opened socket
The veil of skin flapping, the star falling

My face punctured with glass
The teeth eating themselves in dreams

Our blood refusing to breathe, refusing to sleep
Asking the wounded moon

Asking the pillow, asking, asking
How much can it hurt?

THE CHILDREN'S CRUSADE

Crossbow wanted a child,
a little schoolboy with a red hole
in his brow

like the President. He excited
everyone. They made a brilliant
pair of angel's wings from Kaiser foil

and posterboard, they made a little
tufted box. They would cross his arms
on a single burning peony.

They'd get a glossy Testament,
a blanket tucked in
deep around the sides.

He wanted the little boy who skipped
all the way to school. Eve shook
her red head, and the silver

ignition keys hooked in her
pierced ears chirped. "No, No,"
he was going to be

her lover friend. She wanted
someone like Daddy. Archangel said,
"Daddy."

They took stations.
The night hollered through
the branches and the long grass

like a burned TV.
They bit their hands and waited.
Daddy's car closed.

Everything went quiet and they
had to still their heads like they'd learned
when the bedroom door opened.

After they stabbed him down,
Eve came out from
the shadows. She pulled his beard

but only a little came loose.
She stood so tall in mother's shoes,
and with blue and green chalk

on her lids and cheeks,
he never
knew her. He licked his lips

like when he said important
things, and spread his arms
and made his eyes make tears,

he wanted to talk, he wanted
to help them all, but she just pushed
the knife between his teeth.

When he stopped, they tried
to finish. The box was way too small
and he was too heavy.

So they giggled. When they smelled
what he'd done, they giggled
more. A Daddy going ka ka!

They rolled him over and tore
rags of skin from the eucalyptus
and hid him forever.

Now they ran. The shadows
were all gone, and the air
growing as soft as stone

underwater. Underwater or in moonlight,
the hills rose above the earth,
and they ran shedding their caps and bells,

the little silent bells
they wore at wrist and ankle,
they threw away their names and their no-names.

They cast their knives on the absent waters
and their long bamboo spears.
"Goodbye, rusty can opener, Goodbye!"

The houses were snapping.
It was over and they ran. Never
to wait! Now they were free.

LATER STILL

Two sons are gone.
The end of winter, and the almond blooms
near the back fence. The plum, slower,
unfolds under a streaked sky. The words become,
like prayer, a kind of nonsense
which becomes the thought of our lives.

In middle age we came
to the nine years war, the stars raged
in our horoscopes and the land
turned inwards biting for its heart.

Now in February the pussy willow
furs in the chill wind. In March
the sudden peach, cherry, lilac, in summer
the drumming gourd, corn, grape, and later still
the ghostly milkweed and the last laugh.

IV

THISTLES

for George Oppen

A MOUNTAIN THISTLE IN MARCH,
the stem a bitter green,
the blossom faded
like the stained robes
of martyrs.
          Roots
spun through entrails
of the wakened earth
darkening into rocks
and the long nests.

The sun up long
past five, hanging
in a crown of gold.
—Take the mountain thistle—
it said.
          A film of snow
whirling from the thickets,
the new throats
of my fingers
streaked and itching.

IT'S AUGUST.
Dust sifts from the dark wings
of the magpie, the trails
flounder in sand.
A high wind in the tips
of the pines, without
a sigh the leaf on
my palm dies
into itself.
Somewhere
             on this mountain
a truck gears down
and the rocks flake
into smaller and smaller lives.

I CLIMBED NINE FENCES THIS MORNING

haven't seen a cow or goat or horse or man . . .

In the center of a long meadow
try to sit still
the patient rocks staring
the sun stopped in
the pines assembled at the far edge
listening

Each time I lean my weight
on the top strand
something in me tears loose

How do I get out?

IF HE RAN
his long hair would fly
in the wind, if he sat still
his mind would run
with the names of rocks and trees
turned against him.

23 yr old draft dodger
he tracks the rim
of this sullen mountain lake.
He sent his girl away
he watched his Whitman, Rilke, Snyder
go up with the boathouse
a bright showering cage
against the night sky.

He feels the corners
of his mouth pull down,
his eyes vague.
Some old poet
would say, Bereft.
He thinks, Up Tight,
Fucked Over, trying to walk
inside my life.

IN THE CITY OF MY BIRTH

someone sees my eyes
and turns from the mirror
someone hears my voice
and shouts and shouts
to keep it out

At noon through the vacant squares
the sirens breathe
shuddering in each life
I lost

In the room I forgot
which I said I'd never forget
the mended bathrobe slips
to the floor,
the closet sags
with the sudden weights
of regret

The middle-aged press operator
curls on my bed
in his leather jacket
In the shadows
of the struck elm
the sparrows hush

Above on the 4th floor
the Appalachian widow
sings into the sink
until her sons come
one by one
to take the trees apart

DOWN THE MOUNTAIN
in Fresno, L.A., Oakland
a man with three names and no features
closes my file.
> The winds
are weighed, the distance clocked.
Everything is entered in the book.

HANGING ON IN THE MOON SOIL
north of Alicante
where even the rocks
can no longer sleep,
                    the cactus
dreams on the promise
of rain.
        Little pagan
villages of green spines
tenements of earthly joy.

And here and here
a thistle
like a fox leaps
toward the burning
filaments of shade.

THEY GO ON HITTING
flies and grounders.
The darkness rises
from the long grass
and pulls them in.

The last raw plume
of day breaks up
and flares out, when I
look back there's no one,
only a dark sea—

Somewhere out there
forests of antennas,
empty houses, trees, posts,
and cars, all
the closed presences
of this world

And the voices of kids
floating out and back.

My wife and I
stand wordless
on the chilled lawn
waiting for our sons
to come as they please,
to step suddenly out
of nothing, still warm,
grass smeared, robed
in their own songs.

THE BIG GUY RAN AND HID HIMSELF
in the can, and Mez and I
stayed and fought. Their drunkenness
uglier even than ours, their bodies
marvellous and no imagination to pull
their punches.
        Upright to the hospital,
the shabby dignity of losers
who fought for nothing and
deserved everything we got.
           7 years
later the big guy, rabbit-eyed
at quiet New York drink party,
shook my hand.
        Friend, I didn't say,
we get our chance, it comes
round and it
comes round. Those twitch-nosed
academic pants-pisser poets
of the 50's will take up
against the State,
and you'll be with us,
Mother.

RISES IN THE DARK
fixes coffee
hands moving like starlings
above the glowing electric rings.

Outside a mockingbird snaps
from the sycamore
the branch sways
and calms

60 yr old wanderer
he sits in the dark
in my chair, plotting
the next move, the poem

—Tool & Die past,
L.A. backyard cabinetshop
& no loyalty oath
8 yrs Mexico woodlathe—

Always a new dark
the cup nests in the stained hands
the mockingbird returns
the tree returns.

THE DAWN FOX

high on the meth of
drugged chickens
attacks dog, gophers, hoses,
tricycle tires.
        If they knew
he was here they'd hunt
him on horseback among
the abandoned cars
in The Hollywood Hills'
Wilderness, they'd
make a game of it
drinking his death in
Pepsi,
        his death who rode
the shield of Luca up the impossible
Etruscan slopes, who turned
to fight the pig mounted Archers
of the Moon.
        Tearing his
yellowed eyes through the screen door
to get the house cat.

THE THISTLE
torn off and brought down
admired
and tossed on a shelf

All night the jets hammering
above the house
all night the thistle
opening and opening

and now the first sun
flooding

everyone breathing
his own life

the house living

the refrigerator's
even pulsing
the water heater
yawning and
popping

the east windows
rubbed
open on the quicksilver
of the eucalyptus

Not snow but
seeds fallen
through the roof
of my life
on the stained table
the glass
the silent phone
the unanswerable letter

V

DARK RINGS

Young Teddy holds his face
away from the water, tips
his fingers with soap
and washes. The fine hairs
along the jaw darken,
the neck darkens day after day,
and he will not take
off his shirt even to sleep.

———

Who hears my prayers? 8 hrs
plating toilet fixtures, and now
midnight snows on Bagley Ave.
Let the bus come, let the small deposits
of nickel, the flakes of copper
blacken around the heart, let
it be tomorrow. I talk only
to stars, they're coming down too.

———

Between the lost breath
of the fir trees and the air,
a blue smear. Tinged with
yellow, it is a fire
cleaning the way
of sighs in which they name
themselves.
                    3000 ft
below, the day ends in ashes,
in particles of blood streaming
from the eyes of trucks.

———

It will rain today. I waken
hearing the sea, the howl
of old glass against
the wind. The fisherman
upstairs will not get up.
His wife begs, his
daughter cries. The sea wind
breaks again around
my bed with its cargo
of salt, fish tap at
the glass, and laughing
we are underway toward
the black dawning.

———

Heart of the cottonwood
I chopped in October. The red ants
streaming away from the face
of the axe. A dark soft year,
I trace it with my finger, a year
when the grasses turned
downward and poured into
the roots, a year still
in the white yielding heart.

———

All night in
the bus station in Chicago
afraid to go out, saw
a cabdriver throw
a woman into the street, saw
her hat like a circle
of blood burning
the snow, the snow sobbing
out of the mouths
of oil drums. When I stopped at last
in the alley and listened
my heart was silent
and a river of broken glass
moved under my feet.

———

The Bear dozes off
in a dust of stars. I walk
in winter orchards
and the earth creaks
underfoot. No moon and no light
overflowing the black sockets
of the fig. My right fist
pops like a cinder
in the cold. The sun hangs
under the rim of night
waiting for the world.

THE WAY DOWN

On the way down
blue lupin at the roadside,
red bud scattered
down the mountain, tiny
white jump-ups hiding
underfoot, the first push
of wild oats like froth
at the field's edge. The wind blows
through everything, the crowned
peaks above us, the soft floor
of the valley below,
the humps of rock
walking down the world.

On the way down
from the trackless snow fields
where a blackbird
eyed me from
a solitary pine, knowing
I would go back the way
I came, shaking my head,
and the blue glitter of ice
was like the darkness
of winter nights, deepening
before it could change,
and the only voice
my own saying
Goodbye.

Can you hear me?
the air says. I hold
my breath and listen
and a finger of dirt thaws,
a river drains
from a snow drop
and rages down
my cheeks, our father
the wind hums
a prayer through my mouth
and answers in the oat,
and now the tight rows of seed
bow to the earth
and hold on and hold on.

WAKING IN ALICANTE

Driven all day over bad roads
   from Barcelona, down
      the coast. The heat

murderous, the air clogged with dust,
   to arrive at evening
      in Alicante, city

of dim workers' quarters, bad trucks,
   furious little bars
      and the same heat.

I awaken at 4, tasting fried calamares
   and the salty beer the sea
      has given us,

tasting the bitterness of all the lives
   around me in the darkness
      fumbling toward dawn.

My smallest son, on the same narrow
   bed, his knees pumping
      sporadically

as though he ran into the blackness
   of sleep away from all
      that sleep is not—

the dark creased women that hover
   above each soiled turnip,
      each stained onion,

that bleed the bread sour with their thumbs,
   the old beaten soldiers in ruined
      suits, dying

in the corners of bus stations, talking
   in bars to no one, making
      the night roads

to nowhere, and the long gray-legged boys
   hiding their tears
      behind cupped hands.

How much anger and shame falls slowly
   like rain into his life
      to nurture

the strange root that is the heart
   of a boy growing
      to manhood.

It grows in the shape I give it
   each day, a man,
      a poet

in middle age still wandering in search
   of that boy's dream
      of a single self

formed of all the warring selves split
   off at my birth
      and set spinning.

The slate hills rising from the sea,
   the workers' fortress I saw
      bathed in dust,

the rifle loops crumbling like dead mouths,
   the little promontory
      where the deaths

were done thirty years ago, the death
   still hanging in the burning
      air, are mine.

Now I have come home to Spain, home
   to my Spanish self
      for this one night.

The bats still circle the streetlight
   outside my window
      until the first

gray sifting of dawn startles their eyes
   and the motorcycles start
      up, rocketing

down the high narrow streets.
   Teddy stirs next
      to me, a life

awakening once again to all the lives
   raging in the streets,
      and to his own.

Who will he be today, this child
   of mine, this fair
      and final child?

The eyes dart under soft lids
   and open and the world
      once more

is with him, and he smiles at me,
   the father welcoming
      him home.

TO P.L., 1916–1937

a soldier of the Republic

Gray earth peeping through snow,
you lay for three days
with one side of your face
frozen to the ground. They tied your cheek
with the red and black scarf
of the Anarchists, and bundled you
in canvas, and threw you away.
Before that an old country woman
of the Aragon, spitting on her thumb,
rubbing it against her forefinger,
stole your black Wellingtons,
the gray hunting socks, and the long
slender knife you wore
in a little leather scabbard
riding your right hip. She honed it,
ran her finger down the blade, and laughed,
though she had no meat to cut,
blessing your tight fists
that had fallen side by side
like frozen faces on your hard belly
that was becoming earth. (Years later
she saw the two faces
at table, and turned from the bread
and the steaming oily soup, turned
to the darkness of the open door,
and opened her eyes to darkness
that they might be filled with anything
but those two faces squeezed
in the blue of snow and snow and snow.)
She blessed your feet, still pink,
with hard yellow shields of skin
at heel and toe, and she laughed
scampering across the road, into
the goat field, and up the long hill,
the boots bundled in her skirts,
and the gray hunting socks, and the knife.

For seven weeks she wore the boots
stuffed with rags at toe and heel.
She thought she understood
why you lay down to rest
even in snow, and gave them to a nephew,
and the gray socks too.
The knife is still used, the black handle
almost white, the blade
worn thin since there is meat to cut.
Without laughter she is gone
ten years now,
and on the road to Huesca in spring
there is no one to look for you
among the wild jonquils, the curling
grasses at the road side,
and the blood red poppies, no one
to look on the farthest tip
of wind breathing down from the mountains
and shaking the stunted pines you hid among.

BREATH

Who hears the humming
of rocks at great height,
the long steady drone
of granite holding together,
the strumming of obsidian
to itself? I go among
the stones stooping
and pecking like a
sparrow, imagining
the glacier's final push
resounding still. In
a freezing mountain
stream, my hand opens
scratched and raw and
flutters strangely,
more like an animal
or wild blossom in wind
than any part of me. Great
fields of stone
stretching away under
a slate sky, their single
flower the flower
of my right hand.

                                   Last night
the fire died into itself
black stick by stick
and the dark came out
of my eyes flooding
everything. I
slept alone and dreamed
of you in an old house
back home among
your country people,
among the dead, not
any living one besides
yourself. I woke

scared by the gasping
of a wild one, scared
by my own breath, and
slowly calmed
remembering your weight
beside me all these
years, and here and
there an eye of stone
gleamed with the warm light
of an absent star.
                    Today
in this high clear room
of the world, I squat
to the life of rocks
jewelled in the stream
or whispering
like shards. What fears
are still held locked
in the veins till the last
fire, and who will calm
us then under a gold sky
that will be all of earth.
Two miles below on the burning
summer plains, you go
about your life one
more day. I give you
almond blossoms
for your hair, your hair
that will be white, I give
the world my worn-out breath
on an old tune, I give
it all I have
and take it back again.

Philip Levine was born in 1928 in Detroit and was
formally educated there, at the public schools and at
Wayne University. After a succession of stupid
jobs he left the city for good, living in various
parts of the country before he settled in Fresno,
California, where he now teaches. His books include
On the Edge (1963), *Not This Pig* (1968), *Pili's Wall*
(1971), *Red Dust* (1971), *They Feed They Lion*
(1972), *1933* (1974) and *The Names of the Lost* (1976).